Spelling and Vocabulary

Dictionary

1

Author:

Mary Ellen Quint, Ph.D.

Editor:

Alan Christopherson, M.S.

Graphic Design:

Jennifer L. Davis, B.S.

Illustration:

Alpha Omega Creative Services

Alpha Omega Publications, Inc. • Rock Rapids, IA

How to Use this Dictionary

The *Spelling Dictionary* is an integral part of the Horizons Spelling Program and accomplishes several purposes:

1. Students will become acquainted with the format and function of a simple dictionary.

2. Students will be able to see and read their spelling words used in the context of a sentence.

3. Students will have an opportunity to practice their alphabetizing and reading/writing skills by using the *Spelling Dictionary* to perform the following tasks:

   - Look up the spelling words at the beginning of each week's lessons.

   - Record their weekly "Working Words" in the appropriate locations at the back of the Spelling Dictionary.

   - Use the *Spelling Dictionary* as a resource for writing sentences and stories.

Simple parts of speech (verbs, nouns, and proper nouns) are identified, and plural and comparative forms of words are also shown.

A

a   I have <u>a</u> monkey.

about   Tell me <u>about</u> your dog.

add   Will you <u>add</u> these numbers for me?
                verb: add, adds, added, adding

after   Josh will come home <u>after</u> school.

airport   We will go to the <u>airport</u> to pick up Grandma.
                noun, plural: airports

all   The girls put <u>all</u> the toys away.

always   God is <u>always</u> with us.

am   I <u>am</u> going to the store.
                verb: am, are, is

an   Josh ate <u>an</u> apple for lunch.

and   Julie <u>and</u> Josh like to help Mom.

are   When <u>are</u> they coming home from school?
                verb: am, are, is

arm   Julie hurt her <u>arm</u> when she fell.

noun, plural: arms

other forms: armful

ate   Josh and Julie <u>ate</u> bananas for breakfast.

verb: eat, eats, ate, has (have, had) eaten

ax   They needed an <u>ax</u> to cut a path in the forest.

noun, plural: axes

B

back   Will you come <u>back</u> to the house with us?

ball   Josh threw the <u>ball</u> to the catcher.
noun, plural: balls
other forms: baseball, basketball, ballpark

be   Julie will <u>be</u> here at three o'clock.
verb: to be

beaches   Hawaii has many beautiful <u>beaches</u>.
noun: plural of beach

because   The boys were happy <u>because</u> they all received gifts.

bed   They were so sleepy that they went straight to <u>bed</u>.
noun, plural: beds
other forms: bedroom

been   Where have you <u>been</u> all day?
verb: to be

begging   The poor family was <u>begging</u> for some help.
verb: beg, begs, begged

behind   Josh was <u>behind</u> Julie in the line.

big   The lion was very <u>big</u>.

comparison: big, bigger, biggest

bird   Have you ever seen a <u>bird</u> with red wings?

noun, plural: birds

other forms: birdhouse, blackbird, bluebird

birthday   Julie will have a party for her <u>birthday</u>.

noun, plural: birthdays

black   The kitten's fur was <u>black</u>.

color word

bless   God will <u>bless</u> us when we obey Him.

verb: bless, blesses, blessed, blessing

noun: blessing

blue   The baby had deep <u>blue</u> eyes.

color word

boat   Josh and Julie went fishing in a <u>boat</u>.

noun, plural: boats

other forms: boating

boil   Mother waited for the water to <u>boil</u>.

verb: boil, boils, boiled, boiling

book   What <u>book</u> did you read?
            noun, plural: books
            other forms: bookmark

bowl   Julie ate a <u>bowl</u> of tomato soup.
            noun, plural: bowls

box   Josh found a big <u>box</u> filled with surprises.
            noun, plural: boxes, other form: boxer, boxers

boxes   Bob built a tower out of empty shoe <u>boxes</u>.
            noun: plural of box

boy   The <u>boy</u> was playing T–ball.
            noun, plural: boys

bread   Mother baked <u>bread</u> for supper.
            noun, plural: bread

brother Josh is Julie's <u>brother</u>.
            noun, plural: brothers

brown   The dog's fur is <u>brown</u>.
            color word

burn   Be careful not to <u>burn</u> yourself on the stove.
            verb: burn, burns, burned, burning

but   Julie was going on a picnic, <u>but</u> it began to rain.

butterfly   Did you see that Monarch <u>butterfly</u>?
noun, plural: butterflies

C

calling
Did you hear me <u>calling</u> you?
verb: call, calls, called, calling
noun: call: You have a <u>call</u>.

came
John <u>came</u> home after the ball game.
verb: come, came

can
Mike <u>can</u> come over for lunch.
verb: can

can
Joe made a <u>can</u> of soup.
noun, plural: cans

can't
Jim <u>can't</u> come over today.
contraction: cannot

car
Did you see that shiny red <u>car</u>?
noun, plural: cars

cat
Julie's <u>cat</u> was white with black spots.
noun, plural: cats

cent
Mary did not have one <u>cent</u> left.
noun, plural: cents

child   Mother helped the little <u>child</u> find his lost shoe.
                   noun, plural: children

children   All of the <u>children</u> went to the fair.
                   noun: plural of child

chin   Bill fell and bumped his <u>chin</u>.
                   noun

Christ   <u>Christ</u> died to save us.
                   proper noun

Christmas   On <u>Christmas</u> day we celebrate Jesus' birthday.
                   proper noun

church   The <u>church</u> bells were ringing when
                   we got there.
                   noun, plural: churches

city   Jack lives in a very big <u>city</u>.
                   noun, plural: cities

classes   What <u>classes</u> do you like best?
                   noun: plural of class

climb   Will you <u>climb</u> to the top of the hill with me?
                   verb: climb, climbs, climbed, climbing

clock   The <u>clock</u> struck two.

noun, plural: clocks

cold   Eating ice cream made Julie feel <u>cold</u>.
comparison: cold, colder, coldest

cold   I have a <u>cold</u>.
noun, plural: colds

come   Father will <u>come</u> to school with me today.
verb: come, came

cough   Tommy had a bad <u>cough</u>.
noun

cough   I <u>cough</u> all day long.
verb: cough, coughs, coughed, coughing

could   Jill <u>could</u> go with us if she gets her work done.
verb

cupful   Mother needed one <u>cupful</u> of sugar for the recipe.
noun

cute   The little girl with the curly hair was <u>cute</u>.
comparison: cute, cuter, cutest

D

day   A <u>day</u> is 24-hour space of time.
noun, plural: days

did   Josh <u>did</u> his school work before he went out to play.
verb: do, does, did, has (have, had) done

dishes   Bob and Sue did all of the <u>dishes</u> from supper.
noun: plural of dish

do   What will they <u>do</u> when they go outside?
verb: do, does, did, has (have, had) done

does   Ken <u>does</u> all his work before lunch.
verb: do, does, did, has (have, had) done

dolls   Molly has many <u>dolls</u>.
noun: doll

don't   We <u>don't</u> have enough balloons for the party.
contraction: do not

door   The front <u>door</u> was locked when we got home.
noun, plural: doors

down   Jane went <u>down</u> the slide
very quickly.

dresses   Jennie tried three <u>dresses</u> on in the store.
noun: plural of dress

dresses   Mother <u>dresses</u> the baby.
verb: dress, dresses,
dressed, dressing

drop   Try not to <u>drop</u> the ball when you run.
verb: drop, drops, dropped, dropping

drop   The <u>drop</u> of rain fell on the flower.
noun, plural: drops

E

Easter   Jesus rose from the dead
on <u>Easter</u> Sunday.
proper noun

eat   We will <u>eat</u> in a restaurant tonight.
verb: eat, eats, ate, has (have, had) eaten

echo   Josh heard an <u>echo</u> when he shouted into the
canyon.
noun, plural: echoes
verb: echoes, echoed, echoing

eggs   Mother made scrambled <u>eggs</u> for breakfast.
noun: plural of egg

eight   Our cat had <u>eight</u> kittens.
number word

every   Bill wants <u>every</u> boy on the
team to play.

eye   Jill got something in her <u>eye</u>.
noun, plural: eyes

F

farm   Beth liked to spend a day at the <u>farm</u>.
            noun, plural: farms
            other forms: farmyard, farmer, farming

farm   I will <u>farm</u> the land by the river.
            verb: farm, farms, farmed, farming

faster   Jim ran <u>faster</u> than Jill did.
            comparison: fast, faster, fastest

fastest   Jim was the <u>fastest</u> boy
            in his class.
            comparison: fast, faster, fastest

feet   Kevin put red socks on his <u>feet</u>.
            noun: plural of foot

find   Where did you <u>find</u> that box?
            verb: find, finds, found

first   Ellen was the <u>first</u> one in line.

five   Mark ate <u>five</u> hot dogs at the picnic.
            number word

fix Dad will <u>fix</u> the flat tire on my bike.
verb: fix, fixes, fixed, fixing

fly Can you <u>fly</u> a kite?
verb: fly, flies, flying, flew, has (have, had) flown

fly Did you see that <u>fly</u> buzzing
around?
noun, plural: flies

food We took a box of <u>food</u> to the hungry family.
noun

foot David had a sore <u>foot</u> after he fell.
noun, plural: feet

football Jason liked to play <u>football</u>.
noun, plural: footballs

for Will you open this jar <u>for</u> me?

forget Please don't <u>forget</u> to bring the pictures.
verb: forget, forgets, forgot, has (have, had)
forgotten

four All <u>four</u> girls will be in the race.
number word

fox   We saw a kit <u>fox</u> on the mountain.
          noun, plural: foxes

free   The boys got <u>free</u> tickets to the show.

friend   Betty's <u>friend</u> Sue will spend the night.
             noun, plural: friends

frog   Did you ever see a princess kiss a <u>frog</u>?
           noun, plural: frogs

from   Sally comes <u>from</u> England.

G

gate   The <u>gate</u> of the old house was painted yellow.
noun, plural: gates

gentle   The boy was very <u>gentle</u> with the newborn puppy.
comparison: gentle, gentler, gentlest
other forms: gentleness, gently

get   Will you please <u>get</u> that book for me?
verb: get, gets, got, has (have, had) gotten

gift   The picture was a <u>gift</u> from Sarah.
noun, plural: gifts

girl   Bill and Mary had a baby <u>girl</u>.
noun, plural: girls

glass   Sam wanted a <u>glass</u> of water.
noun, plural: glasses

gnat   A very tiny <u>gnat</u> was buzzing in my ear.
noun, plural: gnats

go   Josh and Julie will <u>go</u> to the fair.
verb: go, goes, went, has, (have, had) gone

goat   The dairy <u>goat</u> was brown and white.
noun, plural: goats

God   <u>God</u> is love.
proper noun

good   A <u>good</u> book is fun to read.

goodness   God's <u>goodness</u> is all around us.
noun

great   God is <u>great</u>.

green   Wear your <u>green</u> hat to the ball game.
color word

H

handful John had a <u>handful</u> of wild flowers.
noun, plural: handfuls

happiness The <u>happiness</u> of the children was seen in their smiles.
noun

happy The surprise gift made Ann very <u>happy</u>.
comparison: happy, happier, happiest

hard The last test seemed very <u>hard</u> to Seth.
comparison: hard, harder, hardest

have We <u>have</u> five new fish in our tank.
verb: have, has, had

haven't Adam and Ben <u>haven't</u> come home yet.
contraction: have not

he After Jack fell, <u>he</u> limped into the house.
pronoun: he, his, him

head Judy wore a blue hat on her <u>head</u>.
noun, plural: heads

her   Nancy carried <u>her</u> favorite doll to the party.

                    pronoun: she, her, hers

hide   Can you <u>hide</u> this basket for me?

                    verb: hide, hides, hid, has (have, had) hidden

high   How <u>high</u> is that building?

                    comparison: high, higher, highest

higher   The red building is <u>higher</u> than the gray one is.

                    comparative of high

highest   The <u>highest</u> building of all is the green one.

his   Don sent <u>his</u> friend a letter.

                    pronoun: he, his, him

home   Alice was glad to be <u>home</u> after the long ride.

                    noun, plural: homes

                    other forms: homework

hop   Can you <u>hop</u> on one foot?

                    verb: hop, hops, hopped, hopping

hope   I <u>hope</u> we will all be able to go.

                    verb: hope, hopes, hoped, hoping

hope   We all need faith, <u>hope</u>, and love.
            noun

hoping The boys were <u>hoping</u> to
            see the star pitcher.
            verb: hope, hopes, hoped, hoping

hopped Bob <u>hopped</u> from the house to the car.
            verb: hop, hops, hopped, hopping

hopping Did you see him <u>hopping</u> to the car?
            verb: hop, hops, hopped, hopping

house   Linda and Joe live in a big <u>house</u>.
            noun, plural: houses

hugged The small child <u>hugged</u> his teddy bear.
            verb: hug, hugs, hugged, hugging

hugging Julie is <u>hugging</u> her mother.
            verb: hug, hugs, hugged, hugging

I

I   You and <u>I</u> will go to the store.
pronoun: I, me, mine

I'll   <u>I'll</u> see you in the morning.
contraction: I will

I'm   When <u>I'm</u> ready, I'll let you know.
contraction: I am

I've   <u>I've</u> never seen that book before.
contraction: I have

in   Look for the shoe <u>in</u> the bedroom.

it   When you find <u>it</u>, bring it to me.
pronoun: it, its

itch   The weeds made James <u>itch</u>.
verb: itch, itches, itched, itching

J

Jesus   Jesus is the Good Shepherd.
proper noun

join   Will you join me for supper?
verb: join, joins, joined, joining

joy   Serving Jesus brings us great joy.

joyful   Martha is a very joyful girl.

just   We will be home in just a few minutes.
God is a just judge.

K

kind

Jenny was very <u>kind</u> to
the little boy.
comparison: kind, kinder, kindest
What <u>kind</u> of bird is that?

kinder

I have never met a <u>kinder</u> man that Mr. Wells.

kindest

Jill was the <u>kindest</u> girl in the class.

kindness

My father always treated his friends with <u>kindness</u>.

knew

Paul <u>knew</u> how to bring people to Jesus.
verb: know, knows, knew, has (have, had) known

knock

Did I hear a <u>knock</u> on the door?
verb: knock, knocks, knocked, knocking

know

I <u>know</u> that John will be here soon.
verb: know, knows, knew, has (have, had) known

L

lad   The little <u>lad</u> had on his red cap.
noun, plural: lads

lamb   The little <u>lamb</u> stayed near its mother.
noun, plural: lambs

lass   When I saw her, the <u>lass</u> was
running down the path.
noun, plural: lasses

latch   The <u>latch</u> on the door was stuck.
noun, plural: latches

latch   Don't forget to <u>latch</u> the door!
verb: latch, latches, latched, latching

laugh   I <u>laugh</u> every time I see that picture.
verb: laugh, laughs, laughed, laughing

laugh   Julie's <u>laugh</u> is very loud.
noun

less   Bob had four points <u>less</u> than Bill.

light	Please turn on the <u>light</u> so we can see. noun, plural: lights
light	The box John has is very <u>light</u>.
like	Which picture do you <u>like</u> best? verb: like, likes, liked, liking
little	The poor child had very <u>little</u> food to eat. comparison: little, littler, littlest
lock	Will you please <u>lock</u> the door when you leave? verb: lock, locks, locked, locking
lock	The <u>lock</u> on the gate was broken. noun, plural: locks
long	How <u>long</u> is that piece of string? comparison: long, longer, longest
longer	The black rope is <u>longer</u> than the green rope.
longest	The purple string is the <u>longest</u> one in the set.
look	Be sure to <u>look</u> before you cross the street. verb: look, looks, looked, looking

look   The <u>look</u> John gave me was very funny.
noun, plural: looks

looking   I saw you <u>looking</u> out the window when I arrived.
verb: look, looks, looked, looking

love   If you <u>love</u> me, keep my commandments.
verb: love, loves, loved, loving

love   <u>Love</u> is the most important virtue.
noun

lunch   Erin ate two sandwiches for <u>lunch</u>.
noun, plural: lunches

lunches   Mother made <u>lunches</u> for all of us.
noun: plural of lunch

M

made   God <u>made</u> the world.
verb: make, makes, made

mail   Did you get some <u>mail</u> today?
noun

mailman   Our <u>mailman</u> came at 2 o'clock.
noun, plural: mailmen

make   Father will <u>make</u> a new kite for us.
verb: make, makes, made

many   Jesus helped <u>many</u> people.

match   Can you <u>match</u> the color and the word?
verb: match, matches, matched, matching

match   Dad will need a <u>match</u> to start the fire.
noun, plural: matches

me   Dad will help <u>me</u> with my school work.
pronoun

meal   We had chicken for our evening <u>meal</u>.
noun, plural: meals

meat   My favorite <u>meat</u> is turkey.
noun, plural: meats

meet   Where did you <u>meet</u> Jeff?
verb: meet, meets, meeting, met

mile   Becky and Joan had to walk one <u>mile</u> to the park.
noun, plural: miles

mine   That book on the table is <u>mine</u>.
pronoun

mine   John stopped to look at the old gold <u>mine</u>.
noun, plural: mines

miss   We will <u>miss</u> Susan when she moves away.
verb: miss, misses, missed, missing

mom   Nancy will go with her <u>mom</u>
and dad to church.
noun, plural: moms

moon   Did you see the full <u>moon</u> last night?
noun, plural: moons

most   That is the <u>most</u> beautiful song I have ever heard.
comparison: more, most

mother   Bobby's <u>mother</u> is here to help us.
noun, plural: mothers

Mr.   Did you meet <u>Mr.</u> Johnson at the fair?
abbreviation: Mister

Mrs.   My mother and <u>Mrs.</u> Danver
will help with the bake sale.
abbreviation: Mistress

much   How <u>much</u> chicken did you eat?

my   I saw <u>my</u> great-grandma on Sunday.
pronoun

N

never   He will <u>never</u> do that again!

nice   Helping Sam with his chores was a <u>nice</u> thing to do.
comparison: nice, nicer, nicest

night   Last <u>night</u> the stars were very bright.
noun, plural: nights

nine   Matt's sister was <u>nine</u> years old on
her last birthday.
number word

noise   Did you hear that terrible <u>noise</u>?
noun, plural: noises

not   We will <u>not</u> go to the circus this year.

now   I need your help right <u>now</u>!

nurse   The <u>nurse</u> fixed John's knee.
noun, plural: nurses

O

old   How <u>old</u> is Julie?
comparison: old, older, oldest

on   Please put the box <u>on</u> the table.

one   Take <u>one</u> piece and give the rest to Sally.
number word

or   Will you <u>or</u> Sam go with me?

other   If you take one job, I will take the <u>other</u>.

our   This is <u>our</u> house.
pronoun

out   Please let the bird <u>out</u> of the cage.

over   The cow jumped <u>over</u> the moon.

P

pack   Remember to <u>pack</u> your toothbrush.
verb: pack, packs, packed, packing

pack   He carried a heavy <u>pack</u> on his back.
noun, plural: packs

park   We will have a picnic in the <u>park</u>.
noun, plural: parks

part   Only <u>part</u> of the work was done.
noun, plural: parts

patch   Mother put a <u>patch</u> on the hole in my jeans.
We went to visit the pumpkin <u>patch</u>.
noun, plural: patches

Paul   Jesus called <u>Paul</u> to serve him.
proper noun

peace   We all pray for <u>peace</u> in the world.
noun, plural: peace

peak   Josh and Julie climbed the mountain <u>peak</u>.
noun, plural: peaks

peek   Take a <u>peek</u> in the box, and tell me what you see.
verb: peek, peeks, peeked, peeking

pen   Bill gave my father a new <u>pen</u>.
Jill kept her horse in a <u>pen</u>.
noun, plural: pens

people   How many <u>people</u> will come to the church picnic?
noun, plural: people

phone   Did you hear the <u>phone</u> ring?
noun, plural: phones

photo   My aunt showed me a <u>photo</u> of my two cousins.
noun, plural: photos

pie   Susan baked a blueberry <u>pie</u>.
noun, plural: pies

pitch   John threw the <u>pitch</u> toward the batter.
verb: pitch, pitches, pitched, pitching

pitch   That whistle has a very high <u>pitch</u>.
noun, plural: pitches

plant   When spring comes, we will <u>plant</u> flowers.
verb: plant, plants, planted, planting

plant   Sarah brought Jim a <u>plant</u> when he was sick.
noun, plural: plants

play   Joe and Bob will <u>play</u> football this year.
verb: play, plays, played, playing

play   Sue and Jackie went to the
school <u>play</u>.
noun, plural: plays

playful   The new puppy was very <u>playful</u>.

pray   We must learn to <u>pray</u> always.
verb: pray, prays, prayed, praying
noun form: prayer

present   The children gave Mom a <u>present</u>.
noun, plural: presents

present   Josh and Julie were both <u>present</u> for the game.

pretty   Ben gave his mother some <u>pretty</u>, red roses.
comparison: pretty, prettier, prettiest

purple   Judy's face was <u>purple</u> after she ate the grape candy.
color word

Q

quack
The boy tried to <u>quack</u> like a duck.

verb: quack, quacks, quacked, quacking

queen
Becky played the <u>queen</u> in
the school play.
noun, plural: queens

quick
John is very <u>quick</u> to help others.

comparison: quick, quicker, quickest

quit
Jeff <u>quit</u> reading because his eyes were tired.

verb: quit, quits, quit, quitting

R

rain   The sky looks like it might <u>rain</u> today.
verb: rain, rains, rained, raining

rain   The <u>rain</u> came down very hard.
noun, plural: rains

rainbow   God sent Noah a <u>rainbow</u> as a sign.
noun, plural: rainbows

right   Raise your <u>right</u> hand.
Can you find the <u>right</u> word for that picture?

road   The <u>road</u> was very bumpy.
noun, plural: roads

rode   Jill <u>rode</u> her horse across the park.
verb: ride, rides, riding, rode, ridden

rough   The sandpaper felt <u>rough</u>.
comparison: rough, rougher, roughest

run   How fast can you <u>run</u>?
verb: run, runs, ran, running

S

said   Julie <u>said</u> that Josh would come home soon.
            verb: say, says, said, saying

sail   The boat set <u>sail</u> across the lake.
            verb: sail, sails, sailed, sailing

saw   Bill <u>saw</u> the boat coming.
            verb: see, sees, saw, seeing

saw   Dad used his <u>saw</u> to cut the wood.
            noun, plural: saws

say   What did mother <u>say</u> about that?
            verb: say, says, said, saying

school Where do you go to <u>school</u>?
            noun, plural: schools

sea   Mark wanted to fly across the <u>sea</u>.
            noun, plural: seas

see   Did you <u>see</u> that huge bear at the zoo?
            verb: see, sees, saw, seeing

serve   Jesus wants us to <u>serve</u> each other.
verb: serve, serves, served, serving

seven   Mother made <u>seven</u> kinds of cookies for the party.
number word

shall   I <u>shall</u> see you in the morning.
helping verb: shall, will

she   Jane said that <u>she</u> would help us.
pronoun

sheep   How many <u>sheep</u> did you see yesterday?
noun, plural: sheep

shell   We found a very large <u>shell</u> on the beach.
noun, plural: shells

ship   The <u>ship</u> could carry 200 people.
noun, plural: ships

ship   Mom will <u>ship</u> the package to Joe.
verb: ship, ships, shipped, shipping

shirt   Tom wore his blue <u>shirt</u> to church.
noun, plural: shirts

shoe   Becky lost one <u>shoe</u> at the beach.
noun, plural: shoes

short   Mary's hair was cut <u>short</u>.
comparison: short, shorter, shortest

should   You <u>should</u> be able to see the hills now.
verb form

sign   Al almost missed the stop <u>sign</u>.
noun, plural: signs

sign   Please <u>sign</u> the check before you leave.
verb: sign, signs, signed, signing

skip   Robert liked to <u>skip</u> to school.
verb: skip, skips, skipped, skipping

skirt   Penny was wearing a long, blue <u>skirt</u>.
noun, plural: skirts

sky   The <u>sky</u> was very cloudy today.
noun, plural: skies

sleep   How late did you <u>sleep</u>?
verb: sleep, sleeps, slept, sleeping

slip   Be careful not to <u>slip</u> on the ice.
verb: slip, slips, slipped, slipping

small   Janet wanted a <u>small</u> piece of pie.
comparison: small, smaller, smallest

smell   The <u>smell</u> of cookies baking kept the children home.
noun, plural: smells

smiling   The boys were all <u>smiling</u> at the funny pictures.
verb: smile, smiles, smiled, smiling

smoke   The <u>smoke</u> from the fire got in John's eyes.
noun, plural: smoke

snail   The tiny <u>snail</u> moved slowly along the walk.
noun, plural: snails

snake   Al held the <u>snake</u> very carefully.
noun, plural: snakes

snow   Bill likes to play in the <u>snow</u>.
noun, plural: snow

snow   It began to <u>snow</u> late last night.
verb: snow, snows, snowed, snowing

so   God is <u>so</u> good to us.

softer   Ann's pillow is <u>softer</u> than Julie's.
comparison: soft, softer, softest

softest   That pillow is the <u>softest</u> one I've ever had.
comparison: soft, softer, softest

some   John took <u>some</u> cookies and left the rest for us.

something   Can you think of <u>something</u> that is green?

speak   Mother will <u>speak</u> to Mr. Jones.
verb: speak, speaks, spoke, speaking, have
(has, had) spoken

spelling   Julie and Josh like <u>spelling</u>.
noun, plural: spelling

stick   Throw the <u>stick</u> to the dog.
noun, plural: sticks

stick   The tape will <u>stick</u> to the paper.
verb: stick, sticks, stuck, sticking

stone   John found a pure white <u>stone</u> on the beach.
noun, plural: stones

stop   Please <u>stop</u> writing when I tell you to.
            verb: stop, stops, stopped, stopping

store   What is your favorite <u>store</u>?
            noun, plural: stores

story   Mom read the <u>story</u> of
            Jack and the Beanstalk.
            noun, plural: stories

stove   That <u>stove</u> is very hot!
            noun, plural: stoves

straw   The baby Jesus had a bed
            of <u>straw</u>.
            noun, plural: straw

street   What <u>street</u> is closest to your house?
            noun, plural: streets

sun   The light from the <u>sun</u> shines on the earth.
            noun, plural: suns

T

tall   How <u>tall</u> is Jonathan?
comparison: tall, taller, tallest

ten   Jesus cured <u>ten</u> lepers.
number word

thank   Remember to <u>thank</u> God for everything.
verb: thank, thanks, thanked, thanking

that   Did you see <u>that</u> purple bird?

the   We went to <u>the</u> store.

their   The toys belong in <u>their</u> room.
pronoun

then   When you finish, <u>then</u> we will go.

there   Please go over <u>there</u> and pick up the ball.

they   I thought <u>they</u> were going with us.
pronoun

thick   His winter coat was made of <u>thick</u> material.
comparison: thick, thicker, thickest

thin That little girl is very <u>thin</u>.
comparison: thin, thinner, thinnest

third Sue's cousin is in the <u>third</u> grade.

this Do you want <u>this</u> game or that one?

three Did you see the <u>three</u> bears in the woods?
number word

throw Bob will <u>throw</u> the ball to you.
verb: throw, throws, thrown, throwing

tie John had a blue and
red <u>tie</u> to wear.
noun, plural: ties

tie Can you <u>tie</u> a knot in this string?
verb: tie, ties, tied, tying

time Is it <u>time</u> to go to church?
noun, plural: times

toe Pat stubbed his <u>toe</u> on a rock.
noun, plural: toes

to We will go <u>to</u> Billy's house.

too Jeff ate <u>too</u> much cake at the party.

tooth Will you pull out my loose <u>tooth</u>?
noun, plural: teeth

toss How high can you <u>toss</u> that ball?
verb: toss, tosses, tossed, tossing

tough Jessie found the meat too <u>tough</u> to eat.
comparison: tough, tougher, toughest

toy Nancy gave her new <u>toy</u> to the poor little girl.
noun, plural: toys

tree Can you climb that big oak <u>tree</u>?
noun, plural: trees

trying John is <u>trying</u> very hard to finish his work.
verb: try, tries, tried, trying

tube His <u>tube</u> of toothpaste is almost empty.
noun, plural: tubes

turn Will you please <u>turn</u> on the radio?
verb: turn, turns, turned, turning

two   We will be going on vacation in <u>two</u> days.
number word

U

under   Look <u>under</u> the bed for your sock.

until   Jan must wait <u>until</u> her mother comes.

up   Bob ran <u>up</u> the hill.

us   Come with <u>us</u> to the park.
pronoun

use   Bill will <u>use</u> the new ball for the game.
verb: use, uses, used, using

V

very   Beth is working <u>very</u> hard.

W

walk   George and Greg will <u>walk</u> to the game.
verb: walk, walks, walked, walking

walls   The <u>walls</u> around the castle were very high.
noun: plural of wall

was   Jeff <u>was</u> playing baseball.
verb: am, are, is, was, were

watch   Did you <u>watch</u> a movie last night?
verb: watch, watches, watched, watching

watch   What time do you have on your <u>watch</u>?
noun, plural: watches

weak   When she was sick, Ann felt very <u>weak</u>.
comparison: weak, weaker, weakest

week   Randy will leave for Arizona in one <u>week</u>.
noun, plural: weeks

well   Are you feeling <u>well</u>?

well   Jesus met a woman at a <u>well</u>.
noun, plural: wells

went   Josh and Julie <u>went</u> to see their grandmother.
verb: go, goes, went, gone, going

were   They <u>were</u> happy to go.
verb: am, are, is, was, were

whale   Sally went to see the <u>whale</u> at Sea World.
noun, plural: whales

what   Do you know <u>what</u> to do next?

when   The girls will leave <u>when</u> mother is ready.

where   Kelly didn't know <u>where</u> the surprise was hidden.

which   Tell me <u>which</u> book you like best.

white   The clouds were as <u>white</u>
as new snow.
color word

who   Did you see <u>who</u> went with Judy?

whole   Zack ate the <u>whole</u> pie by himself.

will   Candice <u>will</u> help you.
verb: shall, will

wishes   Wendy wanted to make two <u>wishes</u> when she blew out the candles on her birthday cake.

with   Please come <u>with</u> me to church.

write   Can you <u>write</u> all of your spelling words?
verb: write, writes, wrote, writing, have (has, had) written

X

x-ray   Jeremy had an <u>x-ray</u> taken
after he fell.
noun, plural: x-rays

Y

yawn   Do you <u>yawn</u> when you are sleepy?
verb: yawn, yawns, yawned, yawning

yellow   Daffodils are my favorite <u>yellow</u> flower.
color word

yes   Did you say "<u>yes</u>" to going?

you   What are <u>you</u> doing after school today?
pronoun

your   Don't forget to bring <u>your</u> books.
pronoun

you're   I think <u>you're</u> going to like this picnic.
contraction: you are

Z

zero When it is <u>zero</u> degrees, the air is very cold.
number word

zoo What is your favorite animal in the <u>zoo</u>?
noun, plural: zoos

"Working Words"
Word List

A

B

C

D

E

F

G   H

K   L

O

P

S   T

W

X Y Z